Stephanie Polite

Table of Contents

1. Introduction
2. Steps to Follow
3. Start up Action Timeline
4. Tips to Grow Your Business
5. Marketing
6. Tradeline Accounts
7. Websites
8. Words of encouragement
9. Online or Brick Mortar
11. Wholesale Clothing Vendors
12. Accesory/Cosmetics/Kids Vendors
13. Shipping
15. Tax Deductions
16. Pics
17. Credit Lines & Loans
18. Swot

Introduction

My name is Stephanie Polite, a native of Charleston, SC and I am the owner of TopLine Royalty Boutique. It has always been a passion of mine to either become a nurse or an entrepreneur. After working in the healthcare field as an Medical Assistant for nearly a decade, I decided to pursue my passion on becoming an entrepreneur. I was inspired to open a women's fashion boutique because from my childhood to early adulthood I always felt embarrassed of how I looked. I am a tall plus size woman and society is not too accepting of women like myself. I felt like we were not being embraced in the fashion community. Most people put plus size tall women in a small box when it comes to fashion and expect us to be accepting of it. I wanted to express and show that we are a
fashion icon and trendsetters too.

Steps to Follow

1. Apply for EIN (Irs.gov)
2. Register your business with the Secretary of State
3. Get Seller's Permit (Department of Revenue)
4. Obtain Business license (City or County Office)
5. Obtain Business Bank Account
6. Obtain Business domain/Email (Godaddy.com)
7. Obtain Business Phone & Fax Number
8. Copyright & Trademark (USPTO.gov/COPYRIGHT.GOV)

Start up Timeline

Action: Completion Date:

1. Fianlize Business Ideas
2. Write Business Plan
3. Select Business Name
4. Register Business Name
5. Choose Domain
6. Identify Business Location
7. Check Zoning Laws
8. Set Up Office
9. Obtasin Business License
10. Obtain Business Bank Account
11. Register Secretary of State
12. Review tax requirements
13. Obtain Ein Number
14. Apply Sales Tax Certificate
15. File Trademarks & Copyrights
16. Obtain Merchant Accounts
17. Develop Website
18. Submit Site to Major Search Engines

Launch to the Public

Tips To Grow Your Business

1. Stay Consistent with your brand & Promoting Brand Awareness

    A. Colors

    B. Fonts & Style

    C. Packaging

2. Build Email List

    A. Pop Up Shops

    B. Social Media

    C. Business Cards

3. Understand who your customer is

Marketing

Marketing is the process to get people interested in your product or service. You can do this many ways such as advertising through different outlets. Of course the main platform to use is through social media. Here a list of Marketing companies.

1. Valpak
2. Audio Go
3. Effect Tv
4. Flipsnack
5. 401
6. Addy
7. Soical Media (Facebook, Instagram, Twitter)
8. Yellow Pages
9. Yelp
10. Google or Billboards
11. Local Newspaper

Tradeline Accounts

In order to establish business credit you must obtain tradeline accounts.
These accounts allow you to purchase products and pay back in 30,60, or 90 days depending on the company. Once you payback on time they will report it to the credit bureaus and DUN & Bradstreet

1. **Uline**
2. **Amsterdam**
3. **Quill**
4. **Crown Office Supplies**
5. **Grainger**
6. **Summa Office Supplies**
7. **Gempler**
8. **HD Supply**
9. **Fleet Cards**
10. **CLC Lodge Acct**

Websites

When launching to the public you need to choose the best platform for your products or service. Some of the websites that you can use to develop a website are:

1. Shopify
2. Eccommerce
3. Big Cartel
4. Wix
5. Go Daddy
6. Weebly
7. WooCommerce

Words of Encouragement

NEVER GIVE UP

STOP PROCRASTINATING

STAY MOTIVATED

Online or Brick Mortar

Online: Some pros of online store are:

1. Inexpensive
2. You can design and build a easy website
3. You can follow up with customers/subscribers through email

Questions to Ask before leasing a store:

1. What is included in a lease?
2. Who handle repairs?
3. Can you make alterations?
4. How much will rent increase every year?
5. Is it wired for business & equipment needs

Wholesale Clothing Vendors

1. Orangeshine
2. Fashiongo
3. Shopnouveauriche.com
4. LAshowroom.com
5. LA Fashion District
6. Banjul
7. K Glam (Plus Size)
8. K Too (Plus Size)
9. Rehab
10. She + Sky
11. Pink Owl
12. Signature 8
13. Hyfve
14. Cape Robbin (Shoes)
15. Liliana (Shoes)
16. Chase & Chloe (Shoes)
17. Aphrodite Apparel (Curvy Women)
18. Qupid (Shoes)
19. Wholesale Fashion Shoes
20. Hot Miami Shoes
21. Mir Apparel
22. Giti Wholesale (Plus Size & Reg)
23. Bloom Wholesale
24. Tasha Apparel
25. Magnolia Fashion Wholesale (Plus Size)
26. Sugarlips wholesale
27. Stella Shoes
28. Aliexpress
29. Alibaba

30.DHgate

31.Goodtime USA

32.Hot & Delicious

33.Tic Toc LA

34.Belita Collection

35.Moonosa.com

36.YoungsGA.com

37.Caroline Hill Wholesale

38.Pinktownusa.com

Accessories Vendors

1. Handbagfashion.com
2. Nihaojewerly.com
3. Bluebellewholesale.com
4. Lajewerlyplaza.com
5. H&D Accessories

Cosmetics Vendors

1. pinnaclecosmetics.com
2. eyelashworld.com
3. voxskincare.com
4. botanicalscience.net
5. brushesbykaren.com
6. Allnaturalhealthandbeauty.net
7. luxuryminkeyelashes.com

Kids Clothing Vendors

1. Littletrendsetters.com
2. Poutinpink.com
3. Ladycharmonline.com

Shipping

Factors To Consider When Shipping
1. Weight
2. Location

Shipping Service
1. USPS
2. UPS
3. FEDEX
4. DHL

Shipping Supplies You Need Are:
1. Dymo Label Maker/labels
2. Shipping Scale
3. Poly Mailers
4. Box Sizes
5. Tissue Paper
6. Thank You Cards
7. Scotch Tape
8. Final Sale Stamp
9. Blade/Scissor
10. Sharpie

Tax Deductions

These expenses are usually deductible if the business operates to make a profit.

1. Car Expenses
2. Utilites
3. Supplies (Other than Office)
4. Office Supplies
5. Legal & Professional Services
6. Insurance
7. Taxes
8. Advertising
9. Repairs
10. Travel
11. Rent or Business Property
12. Home Office
13. Rent on Equipment Machinery
14. Meals & Entertainment
15. Depreciation

17

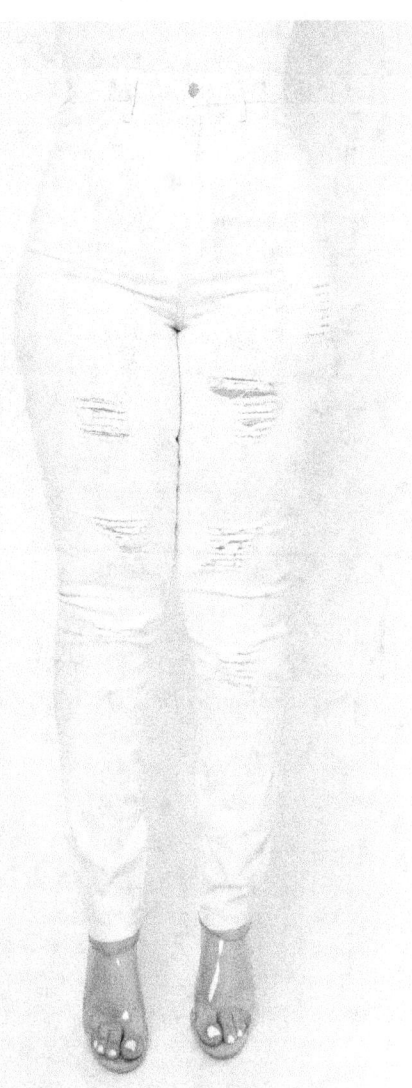

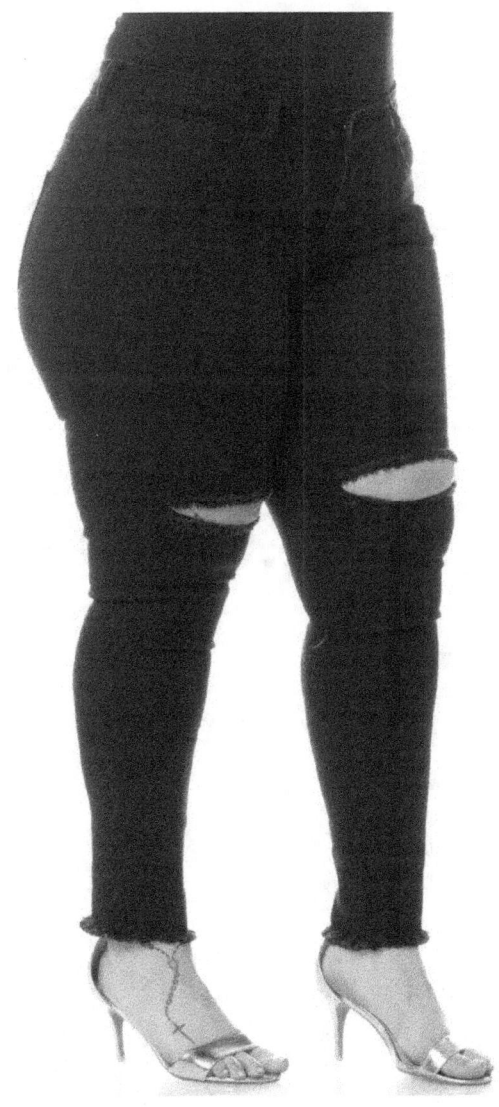

Credit & Loans

1.Kabbage

2.PayPal

3.Square

Swot

SWOT analysis is a strategic planning technique used to help a person or organization identify strengths, weaknesses, opportunities, and threats related to business competition or project planning.

1.Strength

2.Weakness

3.Opportunties

4.Threats

24

You are Now Ready to Begin Your Journey of Opening A Successful Boutique. Always remember to be consistent with your brand. Never procrastinate and believe in yourself and your brand. Your brand is what is most important and it's how people will recognize you and make you stand out from other brands.

www.ingramcontent.com/pod-product-compliance
Lightning Source LLC
Chambersburg PA
CBHW072026230526
45466CB00019B/917